The Magic E

Written by Vivian French
Illustrated by Karen Donnelly

Collins

4

8

9

11

12

15

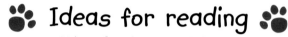

Ideas for reading

Written by Clare Dowdall, PhD
Lecturer and Primary Literary Consultant

Reading objectives:
- read and understand simple sentences
- demonstrate understanding when talking with others about what they have read

Communication and language objectives:
- express themselves effectively, showing awareness of listeners' needs
- listen attentively in a range of situations
- develop their own narratives and explanations by connecting ideas or events
- give their attention to what others say and respond appropriately, while engaged in another activity

Curriculum links: Personal, Social and Emotional Development

High frequency words: I, a, at

Interest words: magic, hungry, tired, thirsty, wet, muddy

Word count: 43

Resources: art materials

Build a context for reading

- Tell children about something that you have wished for and ask them to tell the group about something that they have wished for.
- Explain that the book is about a boy who makes wishes, but who doesn't always like it when they come true.
- Look at the front and back covers together, and read the title and blurb. Explain what a speech bubble is, and that the boy is speaking aloud.
- Ask children to tell a partner what they think the magic egg will do and then share their ideas with the group.

Understand and apply reading strategies

- Read pp2–3 aloud with the children. Look at the pictures and discuss what is happening in the thought bubble.
- Ask children to read pp4–5 with a partner and discuss what is happening, before sharing their ideas with the rest of the group.
- Ask children to explain what happens to the boy when he wishes for a goat.
- Ask children to continue to read the story to p13. Support children as they read new and unfamiliar words.